Pebble®
Plus

T0081402

Life Around the World
Transportation in Many Cultures

Revised Edition

by Martha E. H. Rustad

Consulting Editor: Gail Saunders-Smith, PhD

CAPSTONE PRESS
a capstone imprint

Pebble Plus is published by Capstone Press,
1710 Roe Crest Drive, North Mankato, Minnesota 56003.
www.mycapstone.com

Library of Congress Cataloging-in-Publication Data is available on the Library of Congress website.
ISBN: 978-1-5157-4292-0 (hardback)
ISBN: 978-1-5157-4241-8 (paperback)
ISBN: 978-1-5157-4361-3 (ebook pdf)

Editorial Credits
Sarah L. Schuette, editor; Kim Brown, book designer; Alison Thiele, set designer; Wanda Winch, photo
researcher

Photo Credits
Capstone Studio: Karon Dubke, 9; Getty Images: Opus/a.collectionRF, 7; Shutterstock: Adisa, Cover, Anton_
Ivanov, 21, cowardlion, 11, gary718, 1, imagestockdesign, 13, Ivan Cholakov, 17, Melissa King, 19, thieury, 5,
Thorsten Rust, 15

Note to Parents and Teachers

The Life around the World set supports national social studies standards related to
culture and geography. This book describes and illustrates transportation in many
cultures. The images support early readers in understanding the text. The repetition of
words and phrases helps early readers learn new words. This book also introduces early
readers to subject-specific vocabulary words, which are defined in the Glossary section.
Early readers may need assistance to read some words and to use the Table of Contents,
Glossary, Read More, Internet Sites, and Index sections of the book.

Table of Contents

Transportation

People travel

in every culture.

Let's see how other people

around the world travel.

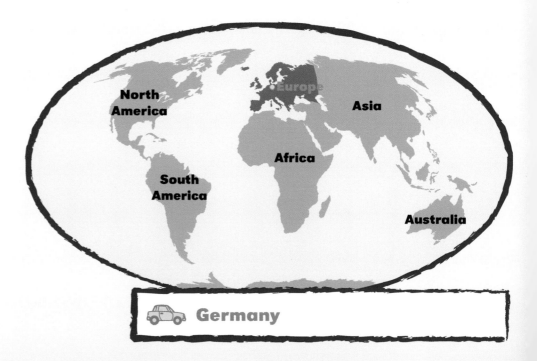

Going to School

These girls in China
walk to school.

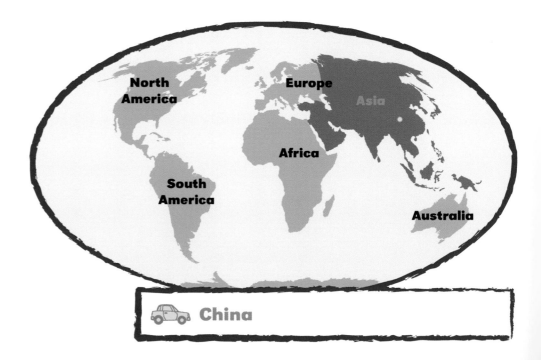

North America

Europe

Asia

Africa

South America

Australia

China

These boys in
the United States
ride a bus to school.

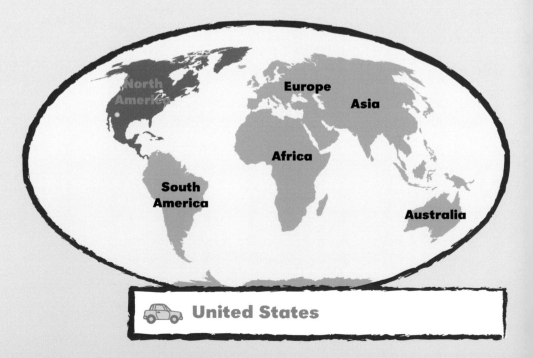

United States

These girls in Japan
ride a train to school.

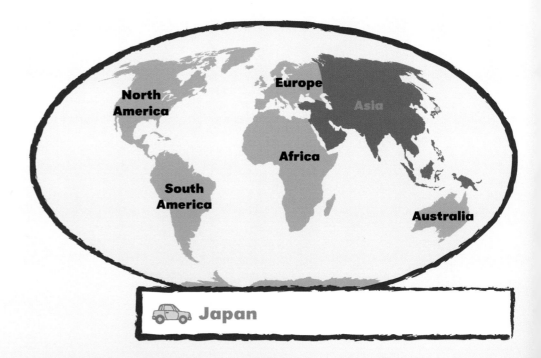

These kids in Cambodia
paddle boats to get
to their floating school.

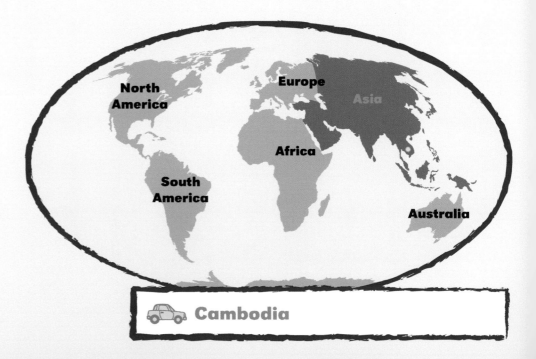

North
America

Europe

Asia

Africa

South
America

Australia

Cambodia

Going Other Places

People in Australia
ride the monorail.

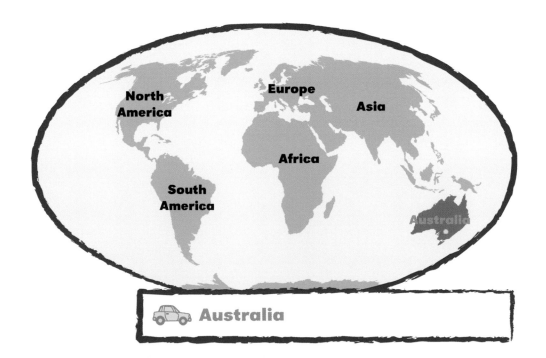

Australia

Travelers in Bolivia
take an airplane
to another country.

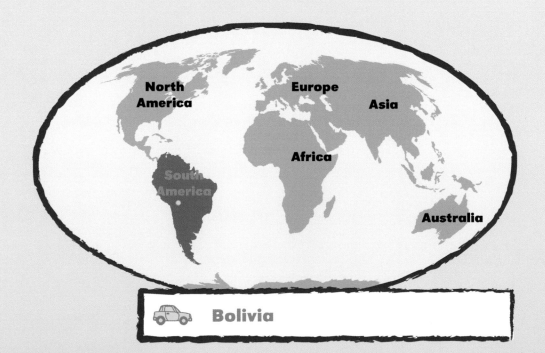

North
America

Europe

Asia

Africa

South
America

Australia

Bolivia

A boy in Canada
rides a snowmobile.

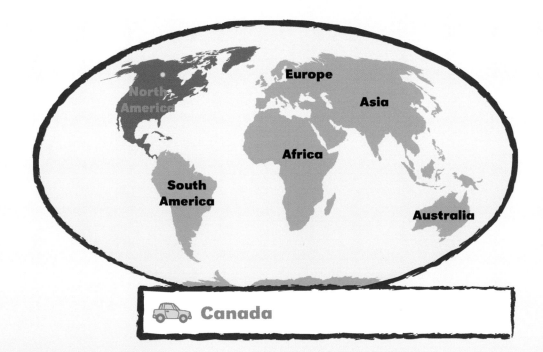

Europe

Asia

North America

Africa

South America

Australia

🚗 Canada

On the Go!

Around the world,
people ride buses, bicycles,
and animals.
How will you travel today?

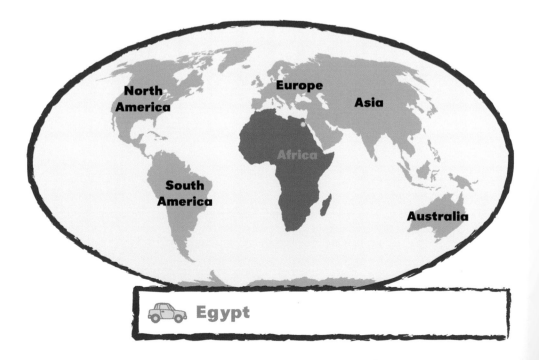

North America

Europe

Asia

South America

Africa

Australia

🚗 Egypt

Glossary

culture — the way of life, ideas, customs, and traditions of a group of people

monorail — a train that runs on one rail, usually high off the ground

paddle — to push through the water with an oar

snowmobile — a vehicle with skis used to travel over snow

travel — to go from one place to another

Read More

Guin, Valerie. *On the Move.* One World. North Mankato, Minn.: Smart Apple Media, 2006.

Mattern, Joanne. *Transportation.* Yesterday and Today. San Diego: Blackbirch Press, 2004.

Weber, Rebecca. *How We Travel.* Spyglass Books. Minneapolis: Compass Point Books, 2004.

Internet Sites

FactHound offers a safe, fun way to find Internet sites related to this book. All of the sites on FactHound have been researched by our staff.

Here's how:

1. Visit *www.facthound.com*

2. Choose your grade level.

3. Type in this book ID **1429617446** for age-appropriate sites. You may also browse subjects by clicking on letters, or by clicking on pictures and words.

4. Click on the **Fetch It** button.

FactHound will fetch the best sites for you!

Index

Word Count: 89
Grade: 1
Early-Intervention Level: 18